The Guitar Masters Series

BARRY GALBRAITH
GUITAR SOLOS

THIRTEEN STANDARDS
compiled by Jim Lichens

Online Audio   www.melbay.com/99902BCDEB

AUDIO CONTENTS

Audio recording by Jim Purse
All photos, except pages 16, 38, and 50, courtesy Don Galbraith. Used by Permission.

Visit us on the Web at www.melbay.com — E-mail us at email@melbay.com

Contents

Recommendation From Don

This collection of Galbraith interpretations provides a very useful tool to the aspiring jazz guitarist. Galbraith's embellishments and substitutions are always musical. And when used in conjunction with the original melody and changes, gives the student a clear and insightful look into the mind of one of the true masters of jazz guitar. We will certainly be using these pieces for many years to come in our program here at the University of Oregon School of Music.

Don Latarski
Head of Guitar Studies
University of Oregon
Eugene, Oregon

Recommendation From Alan

With this publication Jim Lichens has discovered jazz guitarist Barry Galbraith and placed him where he should be, as one of the best jazz guitarists of the 1950's. Though his recordings are no longer available, his printed arrangements of jazz standards have now been rediscovered. Every guitarist will want these selections. Thank goodness we have Jim Lichens.

Alan de Mause

Art work by Pam Parker

Thanks

This book is dedicated to the memory of
Barry Galbraith

Jim Lichens wishes to acknowledge many people for their help, inspiration, and support of this project.

His wife, Jacquie, for her unending patience in teaching him the computer skills needed, and for designing the book's cover.

John Purse for playing and recording these arrangements, and for doing the final music engravings.

Allen Johnson, Jr., who studied with Barry and produced his Jazz Guitar Study Series, helped edit the arrangements and made sure the fingerings were the way Barry would have taught them. Allen also wrote the article, "My Friend Barry" and interviewed the well-known jazz guitar artists who knew Barry.

And to the others listed here, a very warm thank you. Ed Benson of *Just Jazz Guitar Magazine*, David G. Berger, the late Milt Hinton, Graham Cox, Alan de Mause, Don Latarski, Don Galbraith, Neil Janssen, Mike Kremer, Andrew Lane, and Len Williams. All contributed their time and talents to make this project something of which we all can be proud. And finally, I want to thank all the folks at Mel Bay Publications, Inc. They have been a joy to work with.

Book History

Barry Galbraith was not only a very fine guitarist, but he was an extremely good music reader. This enabled him to write out his solo guitar arrangements of "standards" for his students. Both his playing and his writing are very straightforward. What caught my attention was Barry's gorgeous "harmonic mechanisms" (to quote one of Barry's heroes, George VanEps). To this day, after fifty years of playing guitar, I have never seen any more beautiful arrangements.

My partner in "Solo Flight", Neil Janssen, asked if he could video tape me playing the arrangements. Later, he mentioned that it would be good to have a book of the arrangements available for other players. Allen Johnson, Barry's student, and editor of the first four Barry Galbraith books, was recommended to me by Ed Benson, publisher of "Just Jazz Guitar" magazine. Allen was kind enough to offer much helpful advice, and he did a wonderful job of proofreading—I wasn't sure what fingering Barry used, and Allen learned these arrangements from Barry himself. We took Barry's rough, hand-penciled arrangements and added chord symbols, left-hand fingering, and tablature.

Len Williams, in Australia, and Andrew Lane, in Eugene, Oregon helped with the computer topography. Len was also very involved in proofreading.

Since I had done the proofreading for Alan deMause's last two books for Mel Bay Publications, I had a bit of a feel for the industry. Alan has been, and continues to be, a big source of encouragement for me. He also taught me how to laugh when things look grim. Thank you Alan.

David G. Berger and the late Milt Hinton graciously offered to contribute photos from their two books, "Bass Line" and "Overtime".

A real surprise occurred recently. Barry's son, Don Galbraith, who is a professor of biology at Trinity College, found us. This has been very exciting for all of us. Don has written a great article about his dad, and he has provided us with many photos. Don is a big part of the project. Look for his article and pictures in the February 2001 issue of "Just Jazz Guitar". (Ed Benson has included our copy of Barry's arrangement of "Alone Together" in the same issue. Thank you, Ed.)

John Purse offered to record a companion cd for the book. I know of no other player who could do a finer job—John provides us all with a crystal-clear conception of Barry's work.

It is our wish that many players will receive continuous enjoyment playing and performing these arrangements.

Keep on pickin',

Jim Lichens
e-mail: soloflt1@comcast.net

Red Norvo, who was good friends with Barry and Chicago guitarist, Howard Kennedy, told me the following story:

Barry and Howard, who were very close friends, were always kidding each other. When Barry found out that Howard was dying, he flew from New York to Chicago and took his guitar to Howard's bedside in the hospital. After Barry played something for his friend, Howard looked at him with a mischievous grin and said: "Your high E string is flat!"

Barry Galbraith is a premier guitarist of our time. Barry touched all the bases with his mark of unsurpassed excellence! Barry, I thank you for the beautiful music!

Jimmy Wyble

One day Barry and I were in a studio doing a jingle, when a guy came in and asked us if we would like to appear on a "Doublemint Gum" television commercial which was going to be shot the next day. They said it might take all day to shoot it and that we needed to show up at six in the morning with white pants, blue blazers and two blond guitars. He said that they already had the audio tracks and just needed two players to sit up there and look like they were playing. We agreed and decided to bring our classical guitars so that we could practice between takes. I guess it was the only time that either one of us ever got paid for pretending to play the guitar!

Barry was such a great player. I love the way he does the single-line fills in these arrangements. He makes it so easy!

Bucky Pizzarelli

Barry and I were doing a recording date at Capitol Records with a singer that I swear was stone deaf! The arranger had written the strangest part I had ever seen for the guitar. Barry played the part beautifully then turned to me and said, "I wish they would stop writing flute parts for the guitar!"

Barry was a fantastic sight-reader and a great rhythm player. He was also a wonderful soloist. To put it all together, he was a great musician; a wonderful man and I miss him.

Mundell Lowe

I met Barry when we were both part of the "studio scene" back in the 1950s. He was a great sight-reader and was equally at home on the classical and electric guitar. His rhythm playing was outstanding. Through Barry I met his good friend, Julian Bream. Barry also hooked me up with Jose Rusio who was Julian's luthier. Because of Barry, Jose consented to make me a beautiful classical guitar. Barry was on many of my albums and I could always count on his doing a superb job in whatever capacity I had hired him for. Besides his enormous talent, I'll always remember Barry as a modest, humble, beautiful human being. A real gentleman.

Tony Mottola

If one were looking for a guitarist who played superb rhythm, jazz, classical, etc., there man would be Barry. It was always a pleasure to sit next to him in the numerous studio sessions we did together. Among the top jazz players today, there are many guitarists he has inspired. He was unsurpassed as a teacher and coach. Barry was a perfectionist who was diligent in writing out his arrangements and solos and it is my belief that this body of work is the wonderful legacy he left behind for other guitarists to benefit from.

Don Arnone (from insert in JJG article "My Friend Barry")

Barry and I were playing a cocktail party at the U. N. where there were lots of dignitaries including Eleanor Roosevelt. I was watching Barry play a classical guitar solo when a waiter shoved a plate of hors d'oeuvres under his nose. Barry just said, "no thank you" without missing a note!

Once I stayed up all night practicing for a performance of one of George Russell's pieces for a concert conducted by Gunther Schuller. The guitar part was so difficult I just couldn't cut it. At the rehearsal I told Schuller: "Get Galbraith!" He said: "I already tried to get Galbraith. I couldn't get him!" That's when I found out that I had been the second choice!

I remember following Barry in a studio band for some television show. I saw that Barry had edited the music for the guitar parts, crossing through unnecessary notes and leaving just the essence of the chords. He was so good at simplifying. Barry could do it all. Rhythm, comping, solo work, the most difficult reading, tasty melodic lines, great accompaniments for singers. All of it!

Jim Hall

My Dad, Barry

By Don Galbraith

I remember Dad telling me about his first professional gig (he earned $2.00). I think it was in West Virginia, which was close to his hometown of McDonald, Pa. It was a hillbilly band consisting of Dad on guitar, a fiddle player who kept time with his peg leg, and his wife, a piano player who, anticipating Errol Garner, required a phone book to reach the keyboard. From this start, anything would have been upwardly mobile!

Dad was the oldest of three boys who, with brothers Don and Rex, were raised in a multi-generational home in which music was an important though not dominant part of family life. His grandmother played a guitar, his grandfather a fiddle, and his mother was a competent pianist. His brothers tell of how the boys loved to jump on the bed as their grandfather played "Turkey in the Straw". Maybe his hillbilly beginning was preordained! I remember him telling me (confessing?) that when he was a boy he would run home from school every day to listen to the most swinging band on the radio...Guy Lombardo! I don't know how old he was when he began to play, but I recently discovered pictures of him posing with a banjo and with his grandmother's guitar when he was twelve years old. I also found a picture of him at two years of age holding some sort of unidentifiable stringed instrument. I would guess his grandmother got him started but nobody in the family remembers either how or when he began to play. Although he had no formal training in guitar, he did take the train into Pittsburgh for trombone lessons and he played trombone in the high school band. His brother tells of their home being the center for jam sessions with high school friends, including Tay Voye, who went on to play the vibraphone professionally, and Joe Kennedy, the talented jazz violinist, arranger, and Richmond educator. Not bad company!

As a teenager he played around the Pittsburgh area. One of his acquaintances at this time was guitarist, Joe Negri, who remained in Pittsburgh to become THE guitar player in the area. He always spoke highly of Joe's playing. In 1940, Dad hit the road with Red Norvo, the legendary xylophonist. His travels with the Norvo group ultimately landed him in New York where he would spend most of his professional life. In 1941, he played the Famous Door with the Babe Russin band and later that year joined the Teddy Powell band followed by a stint with Vaughan Monroe. Later that same year he joined the Claude Thornhill band until it broke up in 1942 when Claude went into the navy. I remember an episode around this time. He had come home to McDonald to visit when, just as he arrived, a long-distance call came to do a gig with the Woody Herman band. He was back on the train in a flash. The world's shortest visit! He played with the Jerry Wald and Hal McIntyre bands and made a nationwide tour with the Raymond Paige band before he was drafted into the army in 1943. I think he may also have been with the Charlie Barnet and Hal Mooney bands during this time, or after his discharge in 1945, but I'm not entirely sure.

While in the army he played for a short time with a special services band and then he was transferred to the Corps of Engineers. As usual, the army got it wrong. In spite of his dexterity when moving over the frets, he was "mechanically challenged". I remember a kitchen shelf he once installed; anything round rolled right off of it! And my uncle Don tells of a record date he attended in which the score called for a crescendo climaxed by a cymbal crash. Having only a single percussionist, they called on Dad to play the part. Simple enough, right? However, when the moment arrived, instead of the resounding crash of cymbals there was sort of a thup, clank. After a moment of silence, the recording engineer's voice reverberated throughout the studio: "Barry, if you hold your arms further away from your body you won't catch your stomach in the cymbals!"

Following his discharge from the army, he returned to New York City where, in 1946, he was with the Jerry Gray band on radio's weekly Phillip Morris Show. I recall that Margaret Whiting was the female vocalist with this band but forget who the male vocalist was. Herb Shriner was the comedian on the show. I, by the way, was fascinated to see that Johnny, the "caaall for Philip Morrrrrisss" boy, was a real person! In 1947 Dad rejoined the Thornhill band until it became a victim of the mass extinction of big bands, which occurred in the post-war years. I had been spending parts of summers with him since 1946 when he and my mother were divorced, and thought musicians were the greatest people on earth and that there was no better life than being on the road! I don't know how many musicians would want a little kid hanging around but the guys were always great to me. I remember Sandy Spiegelstern, one of the french horn players in the Thornhill band, apologizing every time he let forth with a word that he didn't think was (or should be) included in the vocabulary of a ten-year old. I have no clear memory of what Dad did following the demise of Claude's band but he eventually hooked-up with Peggy Lee and Dave Barbour, and was back on the road again. When I arrived on the scene that summer, Peggy and Dave were settled in for several weeks at the Paramount sharing the billing with the Jimmy Dorsey band and a young comic team by the name of Martin and Lewis. The bass player, Joe Shulman arranged a jam session with some saxophone player and all the musicians seemed to be pretty excited at the prospect of playing with this guy. Immediately after one of the afternoon shows, they set up in a basketball court on an upper floor of the Paramount building. Finally, after they had given up on his arrival, this big (to me) guy wearing a pork-pie hat sort of shuffles in, sits down, takes out his horn, and provides an unforgettable experience. I later learned that Prez was one of Dad's idols and I'm sure he must have really been thrilled, but you would never have known it from his typically low-key manner. Joe Shulman later joined Lester in what was probably one of his last groups.

Few people probably know that when George Shearing arrived in this country he organized a quintet in which Dad was the guitarist. However, instead of the guitar – vibes combination done so well by Chuck Wayne and Marjorie Hymes, the original quintet featured guitar and clarinet. This group never recorded and thus exists only as a memory.

Although some musicians lived to be on the road, most eventually became worn down by the grind. Dad used to like to tell about the time the Thornhill band was nearing the end of a long string of one-night stands and everybody was really beat. The band had just finished a tune but Billy Exiner, the drummer, kept right on playing. There he sat, relaxed, eyes closed, sound asleep! And keeping perfect time! Well, by the time Peggy and Dave decided to come in off the road for awhile, Dad had grown tired of the grueling road trips so he got his cabaret card and settled in New York City. He played the clubs and did record dates but most of his work was as a studio musician with NBC and CBS. Among the shows he did, to the best of my memory, was the Kate Smith show for several years in the early days of television (worth a few jokes but he hated it), the Ernie Kovaks show, "Name that Tune" (a few interesting stories here!), and the George Skinner radio show with the Mort Lindsay band. There were others but I don't remember what they were. During the Kate Smith years, and for several years afterward, he studied piano but the instrument never felt natural to him, probably because it was too mechanical (see above!). He used it mainly for composing, an activity he didn't particularly enjoy, and he later gave it up altogether.

His favorite show was the Ernie Kovacs show which featured Ernie and his wife, singer Edie Adams. Those who remember Kovacs know what a comic genius he was and how creative and even diabolical his humor could be. The show would frequently close with a skit featuring the Nairobi trio, three guys in monkey suits, top hat and tails, ape masks and hairy hands. As the band played mechanical little tunes, the trio would move about like wind-up toys while building a tension that would erupt in some wild sight gag bringing the show to an abrupt close.

Dad always called his mother if the band was going to be on camera - a rare event - and one day she got the call to watch the Kovacs show. So we all gathered around to see Dad live on national TV but began to get a little antsy when the show was almost over and still no band. Finally, the Nairobi trio appeared. The show was over. Obviously, my grandmother had not remembered the correct date. Then, just as the trio's skit reached its climax, the camera panned to the band ... And there was Dad and the rest of the band all decked out in top hat and tails, ape faces and hairy hands! Fortunately, grandmother shared Dad's sense of humor!

Another example of Dad's sense of humor, as well as his patience, involved me as his foil. When I was a teenager I played alto sax (I put it away and went to college when I discovered that Jackie McLean was only a year or two older than I) and would play with Dad when I saw him in the summer. He would write things out for me—mostly Bird's lines and some of the things Lee Konitz (my idol; still is) and Warne Marsh did with Lennie Tristano—and we would play these together. I struggled through them but had a great time anyway. Years later, when I was married and had a family, I received a tape in the mail cryptically labeled "Saxophone Player". I couldn't imagine what it was and, when I played it back, it took a moment to figure out what I was listening to. I couldn't believe what I was hearing. He had secretly recorded our duets and had waited well over ten years to give me the tape! Well, I wasn't as bad as I thought but I immediately understood why dad encouraged me to get an education rather than go into the music business. He emphasized how difficult it was to make a living as a musician, a theme he reiterated when he taught at the New England Conservatory and saw first hand the unfavorable ratio of excellent student musicians to available jobs. It was a lesson easily absorbed because I remembered the time, when he was with the Thornhill band, he had only enough money to buy each of us a hamburg and a drink for dinner as the weeks' pay dwindled away.

In 1953, Dad joined the Stan Kenton band for its European tour. According to Sal Salvadore, the band's regular guitarist, he and Dad traded jobs so that Dad could make the trip. He enjoyed playing with the Kenton band and really dug the appreciative European audiences. But the trip was to have a lasting negative effect on him. Travel was by an antiquated two-engine aircraft into which the entire band, their wives, and all the equipment were crammed. Every takeoff seemed as if it were going to be the last as the plane shuddered down the runway and didn't become airborne until the very end of the paving. The guys felt as if they were collectively willing the plane into the air! They flew through many thunderstorms and the plane leaked water through every seam as they pitched and bounced through the air. There was more than one terrifying moment and the memory of that terror never left Dad. Before that trip he loved to fly; after the trip, I don't think he ever flew again. He happily returned to New York and stayed there, safe on the ground, driving his Volkswagen beetle like a maniac, for most of his remaining years. From the mid to late '50s until the end of his career, he spent most of his time in the recording studios with a club date now and then, one of which, I recall, was with the Benny Goodman band. He did quite a few things at the "Blue Angel" with various artists. He had little tolerance for arrogance and was put off by the "stars" who would show up there to be seen and admired. One night singer Tony Martin strode out of the audience, commandeered the bandstand and ordered the band to play something like "Over the Rainbow" in C. Well the band played "Over the Rainbow", but a key higher, and enjoyed watching Martin crash and burn. The more subtle the revenge, the sweeter it is.

Dad was renowned for his ability to read and, according to an article written in his memory by a former student, Barry Morton of Australia, he was known as "The Hawk of New York". Morton also relates a story in which Jim Hall, having difficulty with a particular passage to be recorded threw up his hands and said "Get Galbraith!" Somebody once told me that he was probably the only guitarist around who could play George

Russell's complex compositions. He had the greatest respect for George, who was also a good friend, and he thought George's work reflected a rare genius. Those who know Dad's work also know that he had a wonderful sense of harmonics. He told me that he learned an enormous amount by playing the guitar parts in the Thornhill band. He said they were often written as if for a horn section and, initially, he had to simplify them so that he could play them. This embarrassed him, but, with an enormous amount of work, he finally got his chops around the music. As a consequence, however, he possessed a dimension in his playing that most guitarists lacked. Young guitar players, take heart!

Sometime around the mid-60's Dad felt his left hand beginning to lose its feeling. Over a period of several years the condition worsened to the point that he could no longer feel the strings. He told me he was playing from "muscle memory". He went to physician after physician, chiropractors, acupuncturists—you name it—in an attempt to find out what was wrong but to no avail. Nobody seemed to be able to figure out what was going on and, though he tried not to reveal it, he was becoming very alarmed. Finally, in 1969, a neurosurgeon at Columbia University discovered, in a set of x-rays taken two years previously by another physician, that several of the cervical vertebrae had bone growths that were pressing on, and destroying, the sensory nerves entering the spinal cord. This condition very likely resulted from the many years of pressure placed on that area by the posture he assumed while playing. He was told that in six months more time the nerves would have been permanently destroyed. He immediately had surgery to remove the excess bone. Although the nerves were saved, the operation not only failed to improve the use of his left hand, it impaired his use of the right hand as well! As one might imagine, the following months were very difficult. He had to teach himself to play again and it was a very discouraging business. It was also difficult to listen to him struggling so hard to regain his lost skills. He would comp for hours with Count Basie records and attempt to play lines he had transcribed from

other guitarists, Tal Farlow in particular. Much to my surprise, and perhaps to his as well, within less than a year he was back in harness, mostly doing jingles, and then he joined the Billy Taylor band on the David Frost TV show. He must have felt that this was the ultimate test because some years later one of his friends told me it was the hardest job in town. He also did a club gig with Lena Horne during this time and an album with the Mel Lewis - Thad Jones big band ("Central Park North"). I think he was with the Taylor band for about a year before he left feeling that he couldn't cut it anymore. He told me that it was just too hard. He continued to do jingles and a little studio work but for the most part earned his living by teaching.

He moved from Manhattan to Queens in the early 50's when he was married briefly to singer Marcy Lutes. He married again in 1957 to Nancy Albam. He and Nancy owned a home in the Jamaica area of Queens, an area rich with jazz musicians. Eventually, in the early 60's, he tired of battling the interminable construction delays he encountered on the freeways into the city so they moved to Irvington, about 20 miles up the Hudson from the city. Finally, around 1975 he sold his Irvington home and he and Nancy moved to Vermont. For many years they had owned a rough log cabin beside a mountain stream, which they used as a weekend retreat and summer vacation spot. They loved the area, so they settled in nearby Bennington from where he commuted to New York to teach and do the occasional recording session or jingle. They continued to use the cabin and chances are if you stopped in on a sunny day, you would find him sitting on a rock by the stream practicing and drinking coffee. This, in fact, is one of my son's most vivid images of him. He also had students come to the cabin on weekends for lessons. A couple of kids drove all the way down from Montreal! And I was floored recently when talking with Frank Varela, a very fine Hartford guitarist, to discover that Frank had been one of Dad's "cabin students".

Dad loved to have his friends up to the cabin to breathe the clean Vermont air and cook steaks on the stone barbeque his brother Don had built. He had a little wood-shed where he would practice if the cabin was occupied but it would get cold out there in the fall. To solve this problem, Don hauled up from McDonald an old cast-iron stove taken from a caboose (his father once worked on the railroad). Uncle Don, who is "mechanically gifted" (as a geneticist, I find the distribution of traits in my family to be very interesting), put the stove together and installed it in the shed but for some reason didn't vent it. Juanita Giuffre tells about the raw October day when husband Jimmy and Dad were jamming in the shed as it poured rain outside. Once she looked out to see Jimmy, head and flute sticking out of the doorway into the rain, while Dad sat inside, comping away, completely oblivious to the smoke filling the shed and pouring out the door from the un-vented stove! Who needs Carnegie Hall!

Dad could play just about anything with strings and did an enormous variety of recording work. He always dreaded the dates that required a banjo but I wonder what he would have thought about the jazz banjo some of the guys are playing now. He did a lot of rock & roll work but I was surprised when R & R guitarist Al Anderson, who was with NRBQ, wanted to talk about Dad's career as a rock & roll guitarist. I was astounded! I knew he did R&R dates - many with kids who were hoping to make it big - but had no idea anybody identified him with rock. It was a short conversation because I knew very little about this other than 1) in 1962 he sent me a photo of himself in a Beetle's wig labeled "My new career" and 2) one problem he had on these dates was getting the "right sound". His big, full sound just didn't cut it. His former student and good friend Howard Collins apparently had the same problem for one day Howard showed up with an ugly green plastic guitar for them to share on the rock dates. Problem solved ... for about $25.

Several years before his death in 1983, Dad accepted a teaching position at the New England Conservatory in Boston at the invitation of its director, Gunther Schuller but he continued with his students in New York.

He would take the train to NY early Monday, teach Monday and Tuesday, return to Bennington on Wednesday, then drive to Boston on Thursday and return either Friday night or Saturday morning. Even when he was ill he maintained this schedule. Sounds to me as if he was on the road again!

In spite of the fact that he didn't think he could play - he told me he had regained about 60% - 70% of his ability - I would have a hard time distinguishing between the pre- and postoperative Barry Galbraith (I'm sure I could have been a perfectly good musician if I had even 50% of his ability!). As a teaching technique, he would copy jazz lines from records, and then go over them with his students. Of course he had to play them to ensure that they were accurate. One day I overheard him playing some Pat Martino lines in preparation for a lesson and if it weren't for the fact that Pat had a rhythm section on his recordings, I wouldn't have known who was who! Nevertheless, he stopped playing when I entered the room. He really didn't want me to hear how "poorly" he played.

Dad was a quiet man, and a private man, not a self-promoter. As a consequence, not much is known by the public about his private life which, of course, would be OK with him. He was basically a shy person who, least of all, wanted to be in the limelight. He was very uncomfortable if asked to play at social gatherings—I think maybe he felt that that would be showing off—a trait for which both his wife and close friends gently kidded him. I don't know if he appreciated how truly talented he was. If so, he never gave the slightest indication of it, always minimizing his skills and praising those of other players. When I was a kid I would ask him who was a better musician, X or Y, like who's better, the Yankees or the Dodgers. And even though I knew he had his favorite players, his answer would always be something like "I like the way X does this and Y is really good at doing that". He was a non-judgmental person who always was able to see the good in a person or a situation. His life philosophy was along the lines of take what life gives you and make the most of it. I've mentioned his patience, which I, as a kid, could stretch to exasperation but never beyond. There were few things he couldn't tolerate unless it was pretension, ostentation, or bigotry and he could spot a phony a mile away. But he could find humor in almost any situation, even his terminal illness. Though he was a man of few words, he was very thoughtful and had a keen insight into life. He was an avid reader and he loved to tell humorous stories. I remember most the great laughs we always seemed to have when we got together.

I would guess that not too many people knew of his love of sports. He was on the high school football team until the day the coach caught him and a friend smoking on the way to practice. He loved tennis and taught me how to play. We always had our tennis racquets whether we were in the city or on the road. I played on my college tennis team and once challenged him to a game so I could show him how it should be played. He hadn't touched a racquet in years but he still beat me! In my defense I should point out that he had recently read Stephen Potter's book, "Gamesmanship", and he employed Potter's principles in such a skillful manner that he kept me either unnerved or laughing uncontrollably for the entire match. He was an avid football Giants fan and for many years had season tickets, along with a bunch of other musicians, until the Giants moved from Yankee stadium. When I came down from Connecticut each Thanksgiving, one of the guys would give up his ticket so I could go to the game. Among the musicians were his great friend Milt Hinton and Milt's wife Mona, trumpet player Bernie Glow, pianist and good friend Moe Wechsler, drummer Mel Lewis—he and Mel would drive in together when they were neighbors in Irvington—french horn player Jimmy Buffington, pianist and vibraphonist Eddie Costa, and a handful of others whom I can't remember. He got hooked on the Giants when they had their great teams of the late 50's and then suffered through the next twenty-years with teams that sports writers describe as "hapless". He could hardly wait to see how they would manage to lose the next game. I always thought it was too bad that he died just as the Giants were on the verge of becoming a winner under coach Bill Parcell's. Although, on second thought, they would not have given him the laughs he enjoyed in the previous two decades.

In his later years he thoroughly enjoyed studying and playing classical guitar and lute. When Julian Bream came to this country, he would give Julian lessons in jazz guitar (according to Dad, Julian loved playing "Honeysuckle Rose") and Julian, in turn, instructed him in the art of playing classical guitar. One of his favorite weekend gigs was to play classical guitar at a Playboy Club that was near his Irvington home. He explained that he liked it because "nobody listens to me so I can play anything I like, do a lot of experimentation, and get a good feel for the room!" A year or so before he passed away, he received a request to come down to the city to play the lute in an ad that was to be produced. By this time he wasn't accepting many commercial things, but the opportunity to play the lute, which had been sitting untouched in the corner for some time, was irresistible. He put the lute in the basement so that it would absorb some much needed moisture, bought new strings for it, and practiced assiduously for the weeks preceding the date. He was really looking forward to this date and finally the day arrived and he drove down to the city, entered the studio, and, as he was tuning the lute, one of the ad agency guys—he was often bemused by the Mad Ave types—came over to him with a puzzled look on his face.

"What's that instrument you're playing? You were supposed to bring a lute."

"Why, this is a lute"

"A lute? That's not a lute! A lute is one of those little guitars they play in Hawaii!"

Well, they sent out for one of those little guitars from Hawaii and he did the date. What the hell, he had already made the trip and a buck's a buck!

Regrettably, as it turned out, the neurological damage was to be the least of Dad's health problems. He was a very heavy smoker and he started very young. He smoked at least three packs of unfiltered cigarettes a day but he must have been at least a little concerned about his intake since he frequently used a cigarette holder equipped with a filter. It is difficult to find an unposed picture of him without a cigarette either in his mouth or burning on a nearby music stand. A memory that sticks with my oldest daughter is the image of his fingers; strong, calloused and stained with nicotine. In the later years of his life he stopped smoking but only according to his own wryly stated definition: "When I finish my pack of Luckies I smoke only one pack of filtered cigarettes and a bowlful of pipe tobacco now and then to fill in the gaps." The predictable outcome was lung cancer to which he succumbed after fighting gamely for a year and a half following diagnosis. He maintained his sense of humor (he attributed his illness to "too much high livin'!") and he had an astoundingly upbeat, positive attitude and life perspective throughout this painful struggle. His physician marveled at his attitude and told me that he was the most remarkable patient he had ever treated. This kind of high regard was not limited to his physician; in many respects his humanity as well as his talent was obvious to those who knew him well. Everybody had glowing words for him as a person and as a musician - how many times had I heard him described as a "musician's musician"? It was a privilege to be his son; he provided me with experiences and parenting, under very difficult circumstances, that I deeply appreciate as an adult. And he certainly left a lasting impression on my children who knew him, not as a talented musician, but as "gramps", who was really mellow and who liked to play the guitar, smoke his pipe and cook hot dogs over a wood fire.

Photograph by Milt Hilton ©

Barry in a recording studio with his Stromberg guitar

Barry Galbraith

(1919-1983)

Barry Galbraith died January 13, 1983, at his home in Bennington, Vermont. Barry (he would not wish to be referred to as Mr. Galbraith), was a member of the Afro-American department faculty for several years. He was a guitarist's guitarist and a musician's musician.

I first met Barry in 1945 when he was a member of the legendary Claude Thornhill Orchestra. The band coupled innovative jazz rhythms, harmonies and melodies with extraordinarily subtle, lush orchestrations contributed by Thornhill and an army veteran named Gill Evans. This combination of rhythmic energy, together with impressionistic orchestration gave the Thornhill band a style that could best be described as "controlled energy." Perhaps it was this style that accounted for the band having the most impressive collection of perceptive minds I have ever encountered. The music, and many members of the group, reflected the yin-yang principle at work. The orchestra seemed to incubate men of quiet strength who had not only a firm grasp of music, but of life, itself. They seemed to already know that music and life are inseparable, and that music is perhaps the most lofty reflector of how life truly manifests.

Over the many years of our friendship, Barry's quiet strength reinforced his dedication to excellence. He is on recordings by Stravinsky and by Miles Davis. He always gave his best on the most classical of jazz recordings (if "classical" means a timeless level of excellence), as well as on a host of symphonic records. He recorded with Gunther Schuller and Billie Holiday, with Louis Armstrong and Itzak Perlman. He did jingles and masterworks.

From 1950 to the late 1960's, I relied most heavily on Barry to make my music "come off." His guitar became a lead trumpet, or part of a saxophone section, or doubled in octaves with the bass and, at times, the whole orchestra. He was a professional in the true sense of the word.

I know that each of the guitarists who studied with Barry during his time at the Conservatory could speak of the personal legacy Barry left to them. For me, he was a brother in the true sense of the word, a role model for all of the nearly 40 years of our friendship. In inestimable ways, he continues to color my life, as well as my music. It is, therefore, impossible for me to conceive of him as having departed. His impulses are still manifesting, so I cannot give a sum total of him. However, the legacy he leaves, particularly to the musical art, is that cultural biases are crippling. In a dynamic and changing world, educators do an injustice by not stressing to all students the importance of their involvement in the rich assortment of musical idioms which this institution offers.

Barry Galbraith was a complete musician; he could do it all. This is the legacy he leaves to us.

George Russell
Jazz Faculty

For All We Know

Arr: Barry Galbraith

Words by Sam M. Lewis
Music by J. Fred Coots

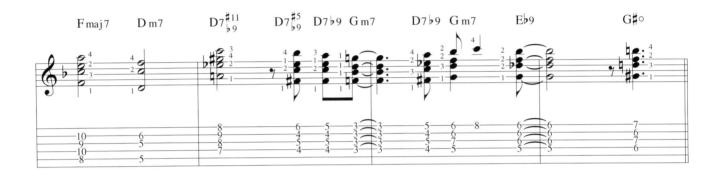

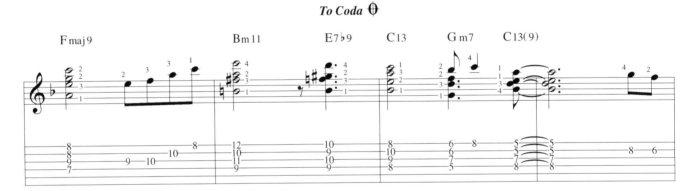

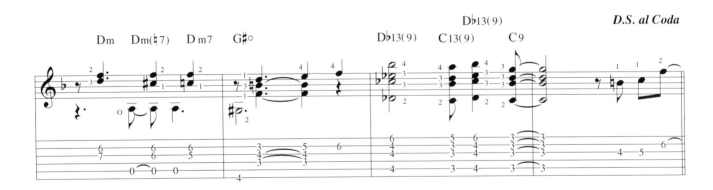

⊕ *Coda*

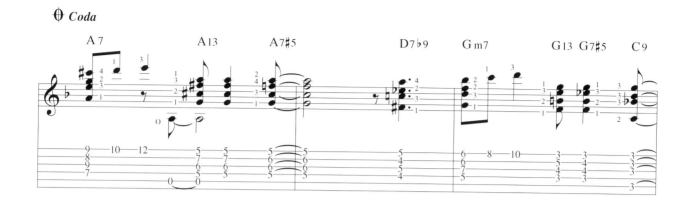

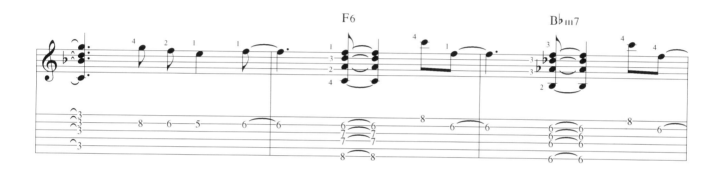

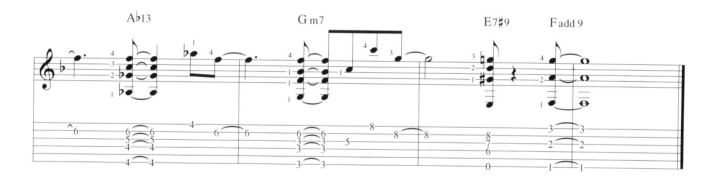

Darn That Dream

Arr: Barry Galbraith

Words by Eddie DeLange
Music by James Van Heusen

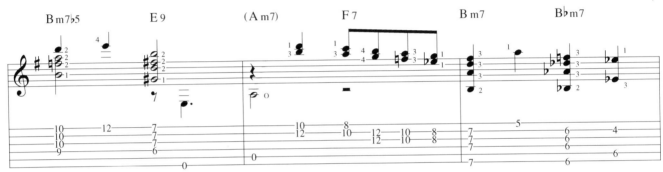

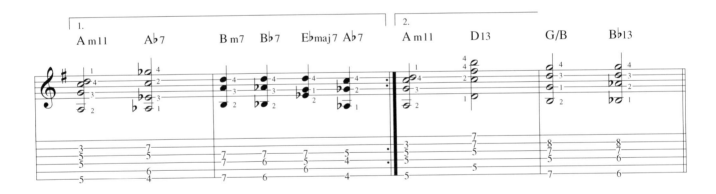

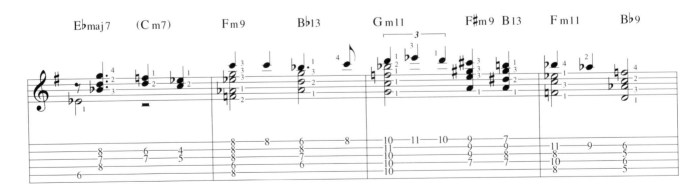

20

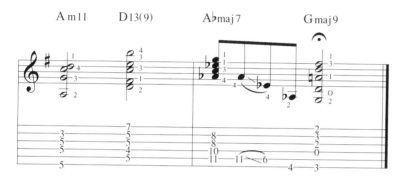

My Funny Valentine

Arr: Barry Galbraith

Words by Lorenz Hart
Music by Richard Rodgers

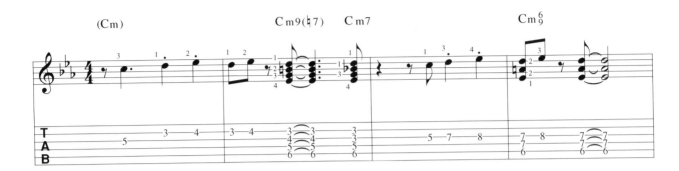

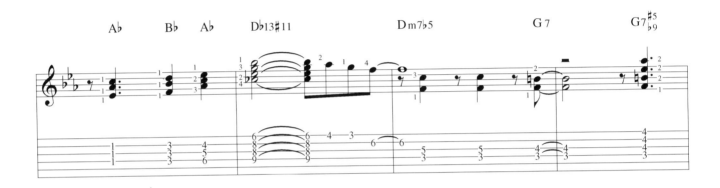

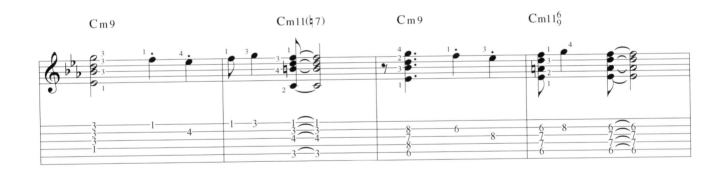

Alone Together

Arr: Barry Galbraith

Words by Howard Dietz
Music by Arthur Schwartz

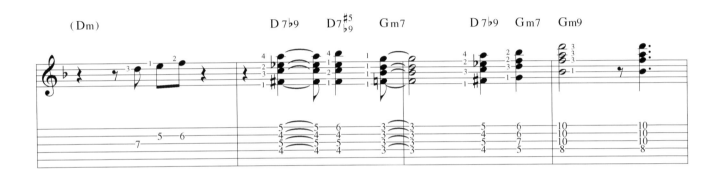

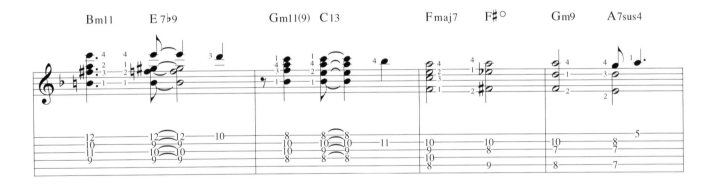

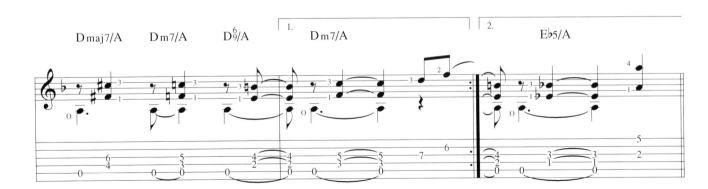

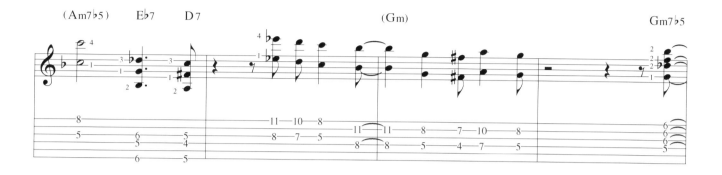

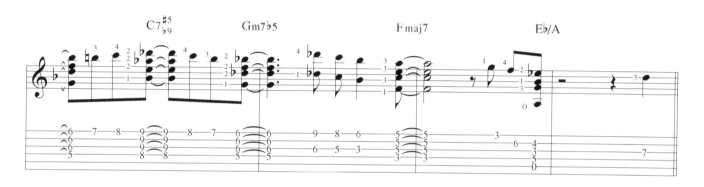

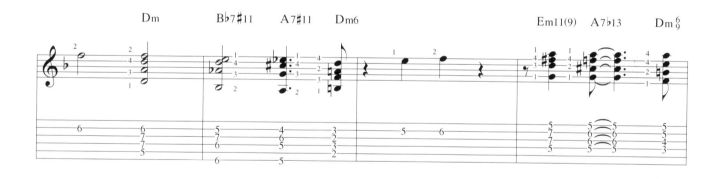

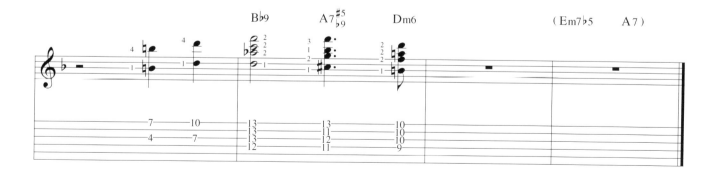

25

I Can't Get Started

Arr: Barry Galbraith

Words by Ira Gershwin
Music by Vernon Duke

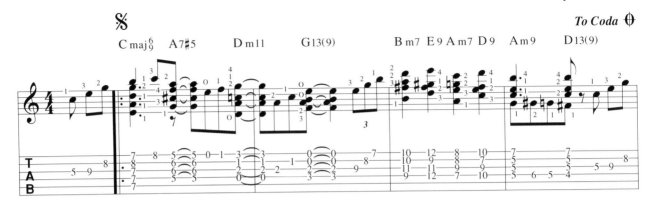

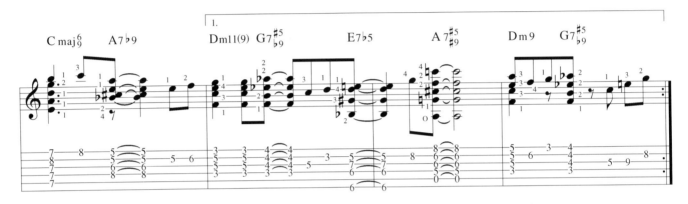

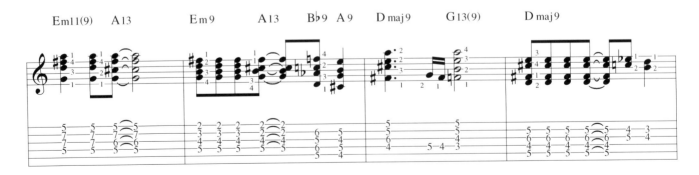

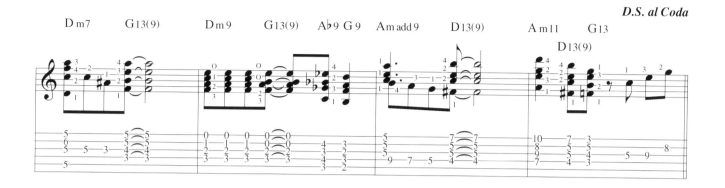

Coda

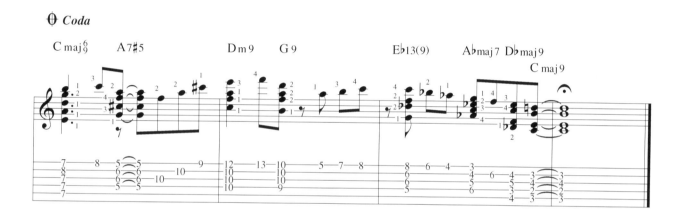

As Time Goes By

Arr: Barry Galbraith

Words and Music
by Herman Hupfeld

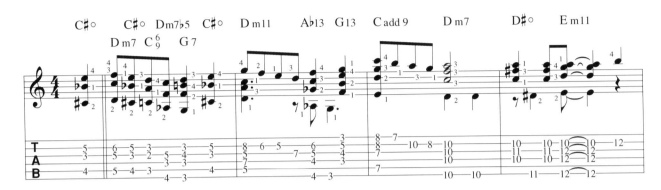

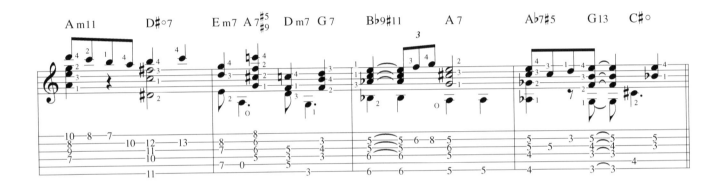

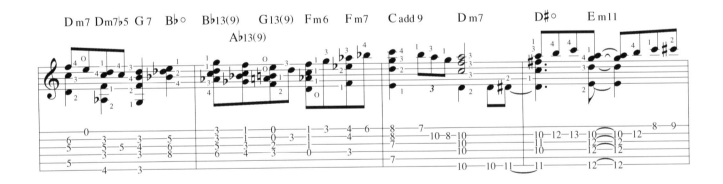

Have You Met Miss Jones

Arr: Barry Galbraith

Words by Lorenz Hart
Music by Richard Rodgers

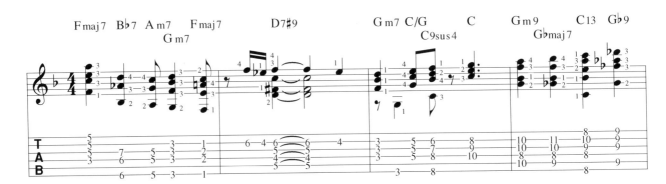

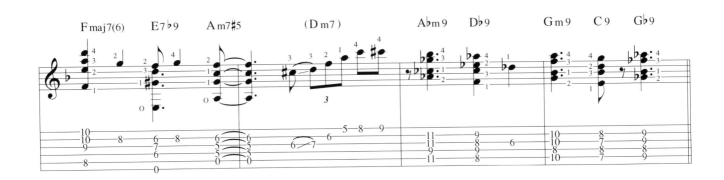

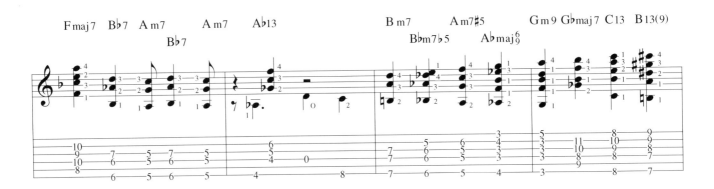

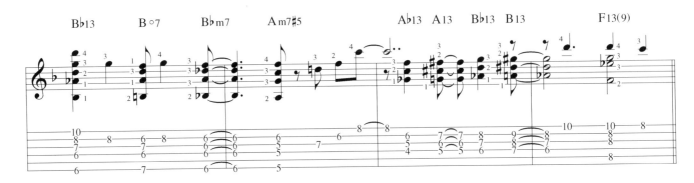

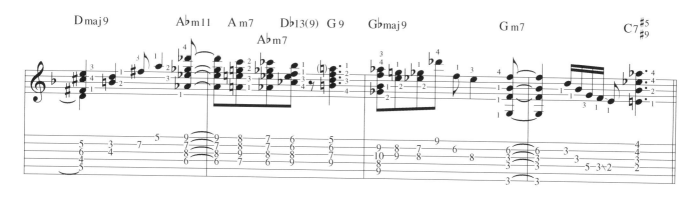

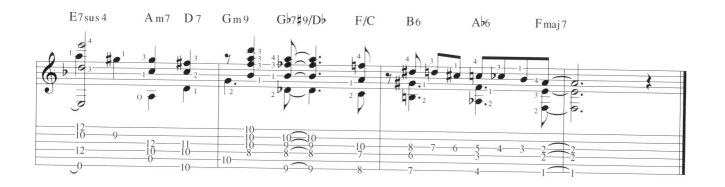

31

Born To Be Blue

Arr: Barry Galbraith

Words and Music by
Robert Wells and Mel Torme

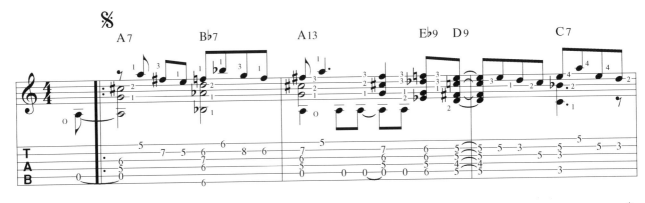

To Coda ⊕

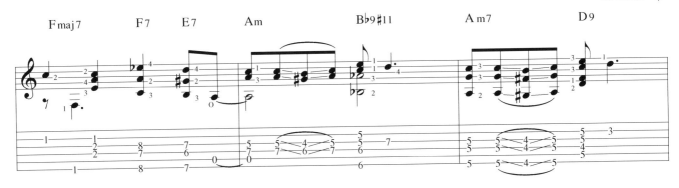

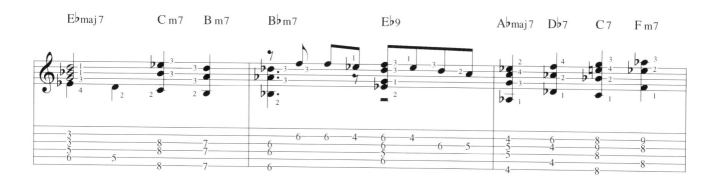

D.S. al Coda

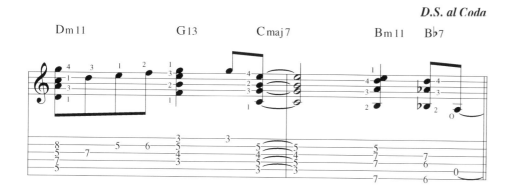

33

Embraceable You

Arr: Barry Galbraith

Words and Music by
George and Ira Gershwin

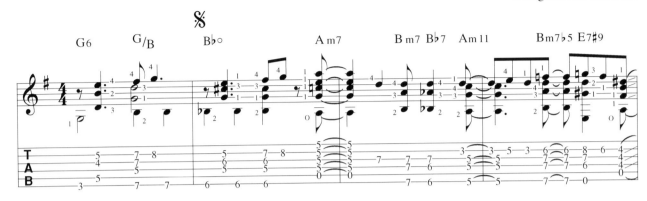

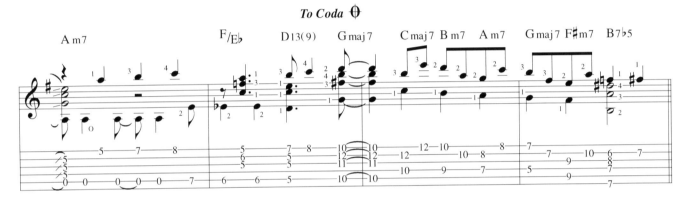

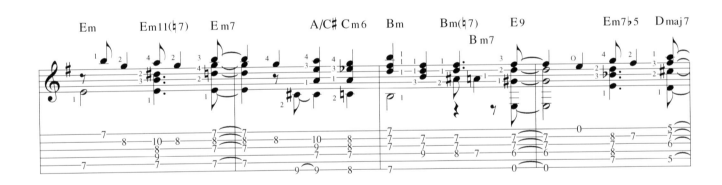

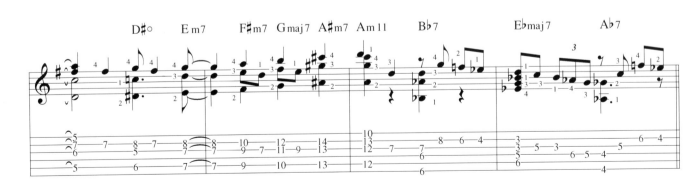

 Coda

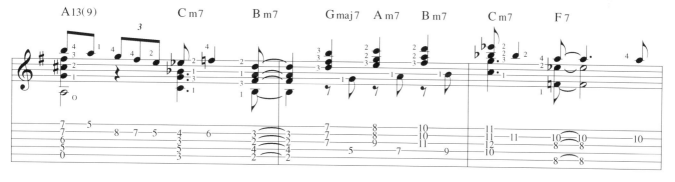

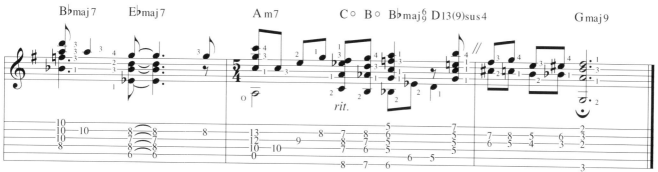

You Go To My Head

Arr: Barry Galbraith

Words by Haven Gillespie
Music by J. Fred Coots

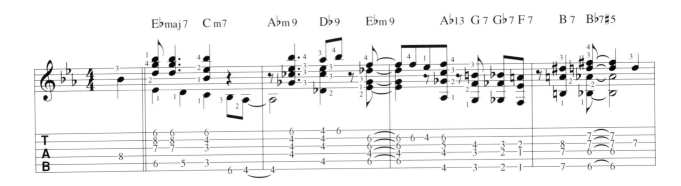

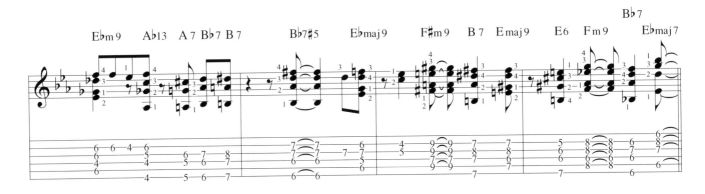

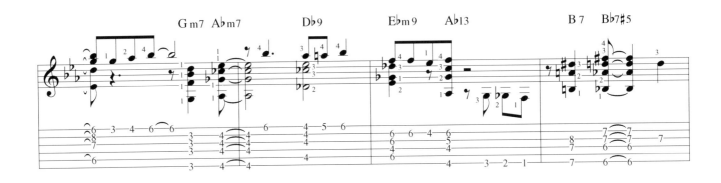

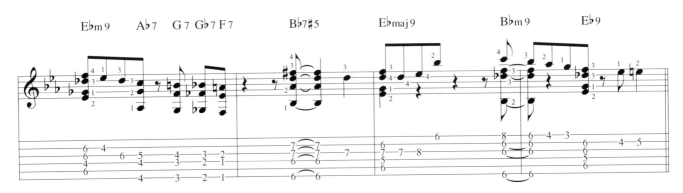

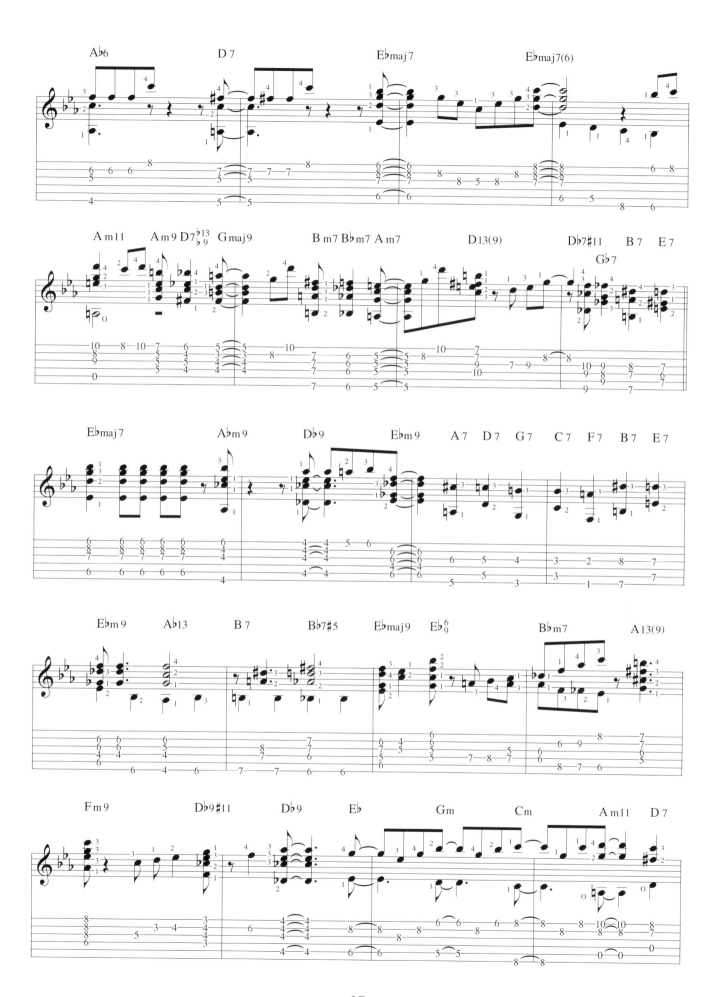

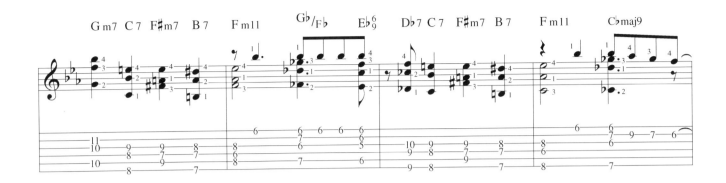

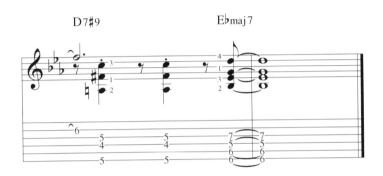

Photograph by Milt Hilton ©

38

In A Sentimental Mood

Arr: Barry Galbraith

By Duke Ellington,
Irving Mills and Manny Kurtz

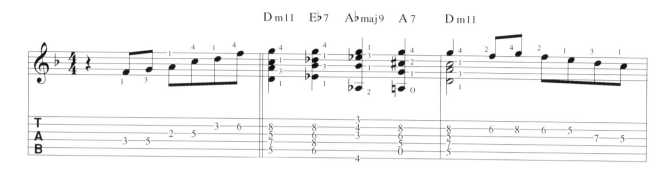

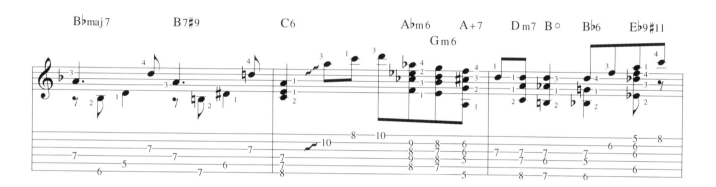

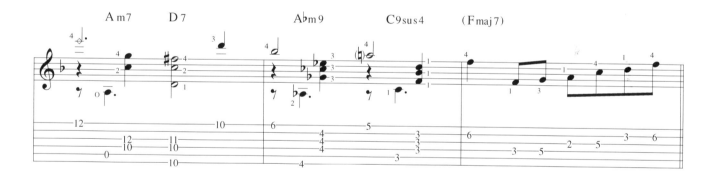

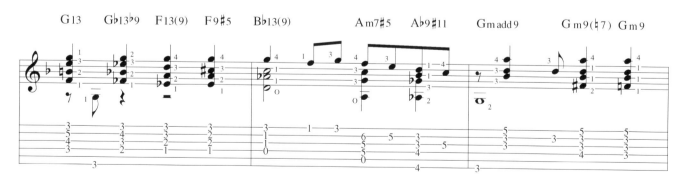

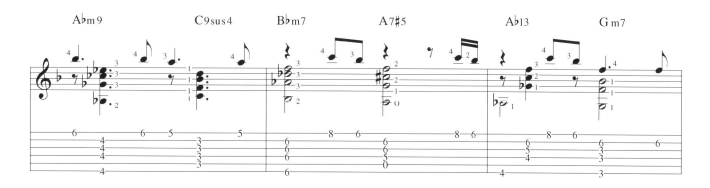

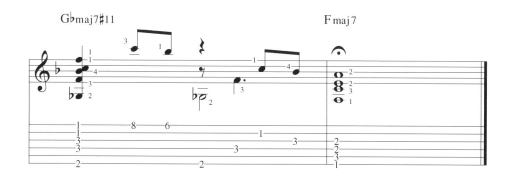

'Round Midnight

Arr: Barry Galbraith

Words by Bernie Hanighen
Music by Cootie Williams and The-
lonious Monk

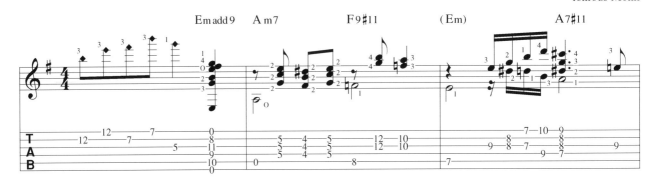

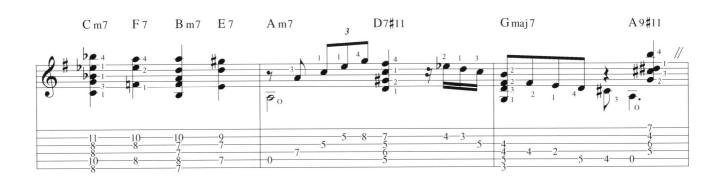

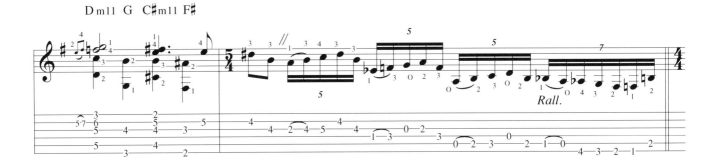

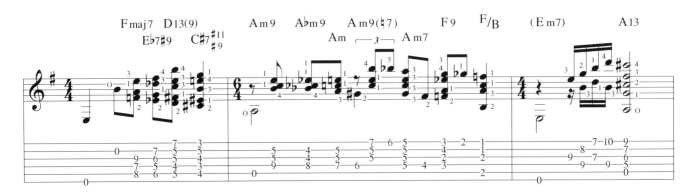

* The C on the first string is played with the base of the left hand index finger.

43

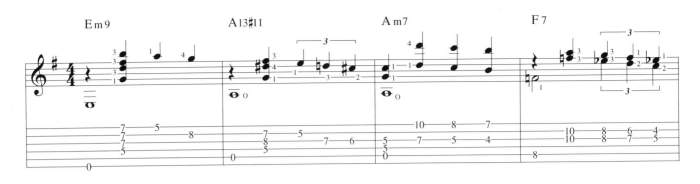

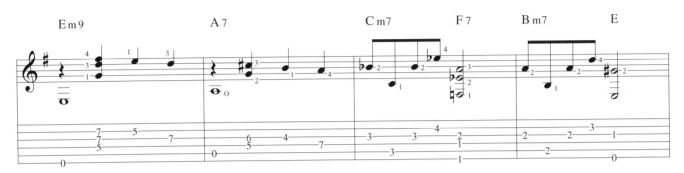

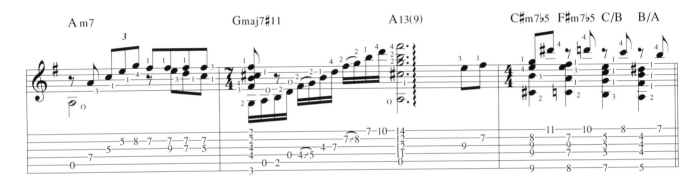

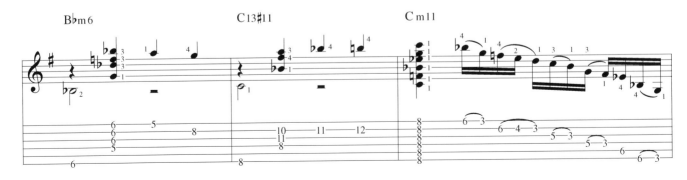

Good Morning, Heartache

Arr: Barry Galbraith

Words and Music by Dan Fisher,
Ervin Drake and Irene Higginbotham

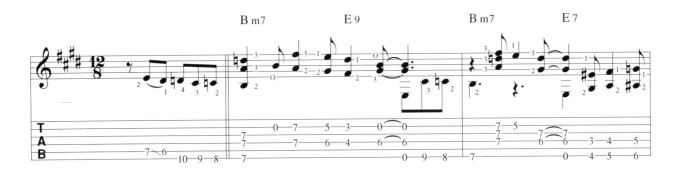

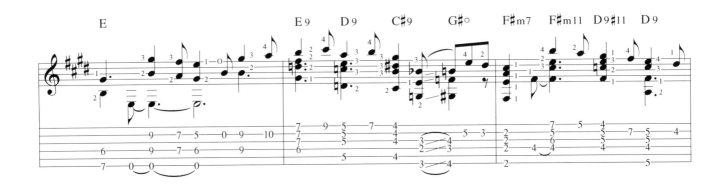

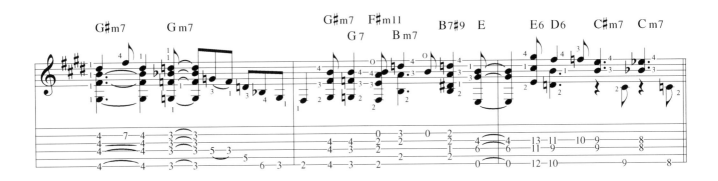

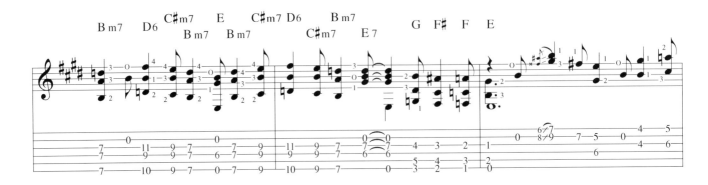

46

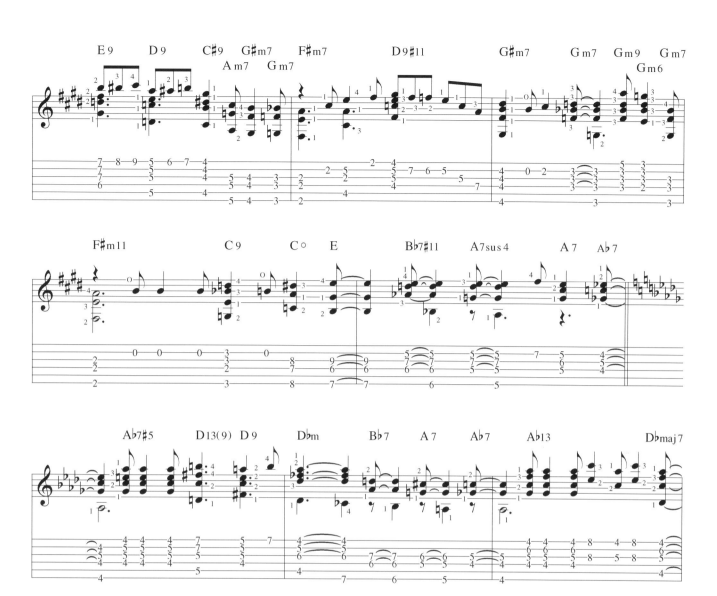

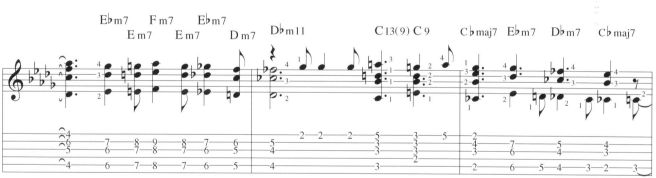

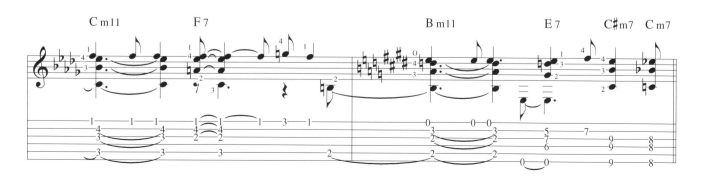

48

Notation Legend

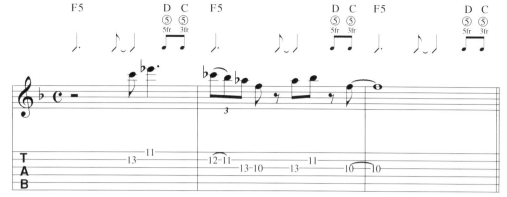

Rhythm Slashes are written above the staff. Use the chord diagrams found at the top of the first page for the appropriate chord voicing. Round noteheads indicate single notes.

Tablature graphically represents the guitar fingerboard. Each horizontal line represents a string, and each number represents a fret.

Slight Bend: Strike the note and bend up 1/4 step.

Hammer-On: Strike the first note, then sound the higher note (on the same string) with another finger by fretting it without picking.

Pull-Off: Strike the first note and without picking, pull finger off to sound the second note.

Legato Slide: Strike the first note and then slide the same finger up or down to the second note. The second note is not struck.

Shift Slide: Same as legato slide, except the second note is struck.

Muffled Strings: Fret hand lies across the string(s) without depressing.

Harmonic: Fret hand lightly touches the string directly over the fret indicated while the note is being struck.

Fig. - Label used to identify a brief figure which is to be inserted into the piece.

Rhy. Fig. - Label used to recall a recurring accompaniment pattern.

My Friend Barry...
Remembering Barry Galbraith

When I was a young man, I had the good fortune to study jazz guitar for ten years with Barry Galbraith. The last three years of Barry's life, I produced the books and records of his Jazz Guitar Study Series. What follows are some of my memories of Barry, his approach to music, the guitar and to life.

Although Barry made a beautiful "solo" album (Guitar In The Wind), he had so little ego that he seldom got himself featured or fronted his own group. Anyone who asks the famous jazz artists of the forties, fifties and sixties, however, will soon find out in what high regard he was held as a musician. If you are lucky enough to have some of his records and a good pair of ears, you don't have to ask anyone to know he was one of the greats of jazz guitar. All you have to do is listen.

Barry was living outside of New York City when I first met him in 1970. I had decided I wanted to study jazz guitar and had asked Jimmy D'Aquisto to suggest a teacher. I had a D'Angelico New Yorker back then. (It was back in the days when you could still pick up a D'Angelico for a few thousand bucks.) It is not false modesty when I say that the guitar was considerably better than I was. It seems to me that I chunked out "Lady Be Good" for him with some changes I had learned as a teenager back in the fifties. This was probably about a third of my repertoire. Barry had serious back surgery and felt it had slowed his hands

down some and had moved into teaching. He taught mostly very advanced students and professionals. I can't imagine why he took me on. Maybe he saw some potential, or maybe he thought something like… "if I don't help this poor guy, he'll never learn how to play!" In any case, he agreed to give me lessons and this was the start of a long and interesting friendship.

I got a real break when Barry moved to Bennington, Vermont. I was living in Middlebury, Vermont and Bennington, while three hours away, was still a whole lot closer for me than New York. I could drive down, have a three hour lesson and then drive back… a long day, but worth it. He would write out enough material to last me for two or three months and I'd go home and work on it.

Barry was a wonderful teacher. While he lived in Vermont, he commuted on weekends to a studio in New York City where he taught with Sal Salvador and Allen Hanlon (his oldest friend in the music business). For years Barry also commuted to Boston where he had the jazz guitar program at the New England Conservatory. He did a killer amount of driving. I was able to see him for lessons at his home in Bennington. Some time I would drive down with Cal McCarthy a buddy of mine (and a great player from Middlebury). Barry would usually treat us to some of his homemade chili and, once in awhile, we would spend the night in his rustic little log cabin in the mountains near his home. This was a great place to hear stories about Barry's career in music. As far as guitar went, he had done it all.

I have a good taste in music but only fair dexterity. I have always had to try to make up in taste for what I lacked in chops. I couldn't have been with a better teacher for my purposes. Barry got me onto scales all over the neck which helped to get me reading, and his concept of chord voicing was the essence of simplicity and taste. Everything he gave me was musical and worth remembering, and everything worked. I remember showing him a difficult fingering I had worked out for some chord and asking if it was good. He said, "Nah. Too hard" and showed me an easier way to grab it. I asked him about Johnny Smith's chords which are difficult to grab, and he said somewhat dryly, "Yeah, but Johnny has great hands." I took the point. Barry's approach was a practical acknowledgment that playing jazz guitar was difficult. Why make it any harder! This was very liberating, very pragmatic. If it works, use it. I quit trying to learn tortured fingerings. Barry never bothered with tablature or chord diagrams. He gave you the music with sparse but logical fingerings where needed. The result was that you learned to read. His hand appeared messy at first, but the way he wrote made so much musical sense that his hand written arrangements were really not too difficult to work out.

"Nah, too hard" was a typical Galbraith remark. Talk about a man of few words! Barry was laid back in the extreme. I think the biggest praise I ever got from him after working on something for a month was, "That's alright, Allen." My respect for Barry was such, however, that such an off-handed compliment from him would make me feel good for days.

Barry made several remarks to me about how hard it was to play jazz guitar. Once he commented on how much easier the piano was. Barry almost never said anything critical about anybody. An exception was Kate Smith, who evidently was a terribly difficult person (and I'm understating!) to work for.

Barry was in the band on her radio show for a couple of years and was so unhappy that he gave up the guitar and started playing the piano. He was amazed at how much easier it was than guitar. The piano proved too mechanical for Barry, however. He found it boring and was drawn back to the more personal and versatile guitar.

Barry was a competent classical guitar player, and once I asked him which was harder, classical or jazz guitar. "Jazz," Barry said. "Not only do you have to play the guitar, then you have to go and make something up!" It now strikes me as odd that he made this remark. Never was there a more effortless improviser than Barry.

The high point of a lesson with Barry was getting to jam with him. He played so great, and his comping made you sound so good. The experience generated enough inspiration to last until the next lesson. I taped some of these jam sessions and later transcribed some of his solos and studied them. They were superb… perfect, complete mini-compositions.

Barry pointed out that many classical musicians couldn't improvise. One exception, who Barry greatly admired, was Julian Bream. He was Barry's favorite classical player. Barry said he played with tremendous intensity. Barry was friends with Bream and told me a story about jamming with him one night at a party. They were both drinking and as the evening wore on, Barry said that no matter what song they started out on they always ended up on "Making Mischief With You!" Though Barry didn't drink much when I knew him, I am sure he did his share as a young man.

Even though I produced Barry's Jazz Guitar Study Series, I was never able to get really complete biographical information about him. He just wasn't interested in documenting his past. It is known that in the early forties, he performed with Art Tatum, Hal McIntyre, band-leader Teddy Powell and Red Norvo. A highlight in Barry's career was playing with Claude Thornhill. He was in the Thornhill band both before and after an army stint during World War II. He toured with Stan Kenton in 1953 and accompanied Peggy Lee but gradually moved into studio work. As a top guitarist of the fifties and sixties, a list of who Barry recorded with would be a who's who of jazz and popular music including such names as Bucky Pizzarelli, Benny Goodman, Gil Evans, Tony Bennett, Ella Fitzgerald and Tal Farlow. Another highlight in Barry's career was the work he did for George Russell.

When George got ready to record one of his intricate jazz compositions, he would call on Barry for the guitar part. Barry told me that George's music was the most challenging music he ever played on the guitar. He and George admired each other greatly. In fact, when Barry died, he left all of his music to George. I suspect that Barry may have been the only jazz guitar player who could have sat down and read George Russell's music at a recording session. For years, Barry was the guy they called in if there was trouble with a difficult guitar part in a recording session. Jimmy D'Aquisto told me a funny story that relates to Barry's reputation as a trouble shooter.

For some reason Jimmy was at one of Barry's recording sessions. When they were on a break, Jimmy and Barry went into the next studio where another session was going on that included four top guitarists. I believe the names Jimmy mentioned were Tony Mottola, Bucky Pizzarelli, Don Arnone and Vinnie Bell. Anyway, evidently the session was not going well because Jimmy said it was really funny to see the look on these guy's faces when they saw Barry walk in. According to Jimmy, Barry said, "Relax fellas, I'm just visiting!"

For years, Barry was a member of a group of studio players known informally as the New York Rhythm Section. These four guys were Barry, Hank Jones on piano, Osie Johnson on drums and Milt Hinton on bass. Once again, when there was a really difficult session to be done, this was the group that got called in. They were on hundreds of albums. Everything from pop to the most sophisticated jazz. Milt Hinton and Barry were

really good friends. A couple of years ago I bumped into Milt at the Atlanta Jazz Party and went up to introduce myself. I stuck out my hand and said, "Are you Mr. Hinton?" He said, "Naw, I'm Milt!"

When he found out that I was a friend of Barry's, he said, "Any friend of Barry's is a friend of mine!" We were soon reminiscing about our mutual friend, and he told me the following story:

Evidently Milt had a really bad automobile accident when, as a young man, he was driving for Al Capone in Chicago. (The accident may have been a blessing in disguise because I doubt if a career working for Capone would have been as productive for Milt as music provided to be.) The accident upset Milt so much that he refused to drive again, and since Milt and Barry both lived on Long Island, Barry used to drive him to and from recording sessions. The funny thing was that Barry had a yellow Volkswagon Beetle. Milt said that they would come out of the studio about eleven at night and start to load up. He said that by the time they got Barry's guitar and amp in the car and Milt's bass and had managed to crawl in themselves, there would usually be a small crowd on the sidewalk watching their contortions. Milt would stick his head out of the car as they drove off and say, "Now we're going 'round the corner and pick up the drummer!"

Barry's taste ran to playing very sophisticated music. Interestingly, the jazz player he most admired was Charlie Christian. He said that Christian's solos were brilliant and completely "unstudied." Though Barry admired many other players such as Tal Farlow (with whom he made an album) and Jimmy Raney, when it came down to listening to jazz guitar records, Barry, like me, usually wound up with Wes Montgomery or Jim Hall. He knew many of the great players personally. He said that Jack Marshall was one of the funniest jazz guitar players he ever met. According to Barry, Jack made the classic remark that ought to tickle every jazz guitar player. "The trouble with life is, it just doesn't lay right."

Barry also greatly admired players who were not guitar players. Two who come to mind are Bill Evans and Lester Young. Knowing I would never have great chops, Barry encouraged me to try to play more lyrical solos. He told me to listen to Lester Young. Barry said that when Lester Young first recorded "These Foolish Things" it had a huge impact on the jazz world. Barry said, "All of us went around trying to figure out how to do what Lester had done in that solo." He warned me that the trouble was that Lester recorded with some pretty bad groups and that you had to wade through a lot of junk to hear Lester's good stuff.

Barry's own sense of humor was wonderfully dry and laid back and would pop up in unexpected ways. Once he wrote an end-chord on a chord solo he had written out for me to learn. The chord stretched over five frets on the lower part of the neck with a high E on the first string at the twelfth fret... impossible to play, but he had written in the fingering. Over the top note he had written "nose!"

Barry was a great admirer of Stromberg guitars. He once told me that he was responsible for introducing them into Nashville when he showed his Stromberg to Hank Garland and Hank ordered one. As jazz guitar became more and more amplified, Barry moved with the times. When I knew him, he was getting a wonderful acoustic-type sound playing an old Guild laminated archtop through a Polytone amp with a fifteen inch speaker. He liked an extra wide neck and would use no effects, not even reverb.

Around 1980, Barry helped when I brought Jimmy D'Aquisto to Vermont to work with Roger Borys in perfecting Roger's laminated jazz archtop: the B-120 (see drawing on page 30 of JJG's February '96 issue). Judging by the number of pros who now use the B-120, Roger, Jimmy and Barry really came up with something.

One of the accomplishments of my life which gives me great satisfaction is the production of Barry's Jazz Guitar Study Series. There are more well-known players than Barry, but due to his broad playing and teaching experience and the way his mind worked, nobody, and I mean nobody, had his clear understanding of jazz guitar. By encouraging him to write his study series and by producing it and assuring its continuing distribution, I know I have preserved some extremely valuable musical knowledge that would have otherwise been lost. All of the books and records of the series are good (there are five books and three CDs), but book III, The Guitar Comping book (and CD with Milt Hinton) is the definitive study of jazz guitar comping. If this claim sounds extravagant, all you have to do is listen to the CD, better yet, play along with it. You will quickly come to agree with me.

Another good thing is that working on the study series allowed Barry to remain productive even after his health failed. He finished the series not too long before he died.

My little publishing company was not capable of doing a good enough job of distributing Barry's books and records, so shortly after he died, I decided to sell the series to Jamey Aebersold. Jamey has done a good job with the series. I no longer have any financial interest in the study series. The satisfaction of keeping it available meant more to me than maintaining ownership. Anyone who wants to order any of Barry's books and/or CDs can do so through Jamey Aebersold, P.O. Box 1244, New Albany, IN 47151-1244 or call toll free: 800-456-1388.

Barry was more than admired. He would be embarrassed to hear this but he was loved. He was a combination of so many wonderful qualities-innate kindness, humor and lack of ego, not to mention all that talent and knowledge. All of us who knew him feel very, very lucky.

Allen Johnson, Jr.
406 Cherry St. Mountain Brook, AL 35213

PS. I would love to hear from anyone who wants to share a story about Barry.

Artist / Album	Title	Label
Cannonball Adderly Sextet	Jump for Joy	Mercury MG-20530
After Hours Jazz		Epic 3339
Manny Albam	Manny Albam Orchestra	Victor G4JB-6028
	Brass on Fire	Solid State 18000
David Allen Sings Jerome Kern		World Pacific WPM-408
The Baroque Jazz Quartet	Jazz for Bach Buffs	Realm –B9245
Basses Loaded		Atlantic 1272
Tony Bennett	Snowfall	Columbia 9439
John Benson Brooks	Folk Jazz, U.S.A.	Vik LX-1083
	Alabama Concerto	Riverside RLP-1123
	Reissued on CD	Fantasy/Jazz Classics
	B000000Z7Q	
Eddie Bert	East Coast Sounds	Jazztone J1276
	Let's Dig Bert	Trans-World 208
	Modern Moods	Jazztone J-1223
Bix, Fats, Duke		Atlantic 1250
The Brothers		Victor LPM-1162
Ruby Braff	Blowing Around the World	United Artists UA-3045
Clifford Brown With Strings		EmArcy EXPR-1011
Ralph Burns	The Masters Revisited	Decca DL-8555
	Very Warm For Jazz	Decca DL-9207
	Porgy and Bess	Decca DL-79215
	Title unknown	? ? AQ-710
The Best of Kenny Burrell		Prestige 7448
Tony Cabot	College Sings	Victor 1308
		Victor 1309
		Victor 1310
Jimmy Cleveland All Stars		EmArcy 36066
Michael Coldin Septet	Sillouettes in Jazz	Everest SDBR 1038
Chris Conner	Chris Conner	Atlantic 1228
Mel Davis		Epic 3268
Bobby Dukof	Tender Sax	Victor LPM-1446
		Victor LPM-1166
		Victor LPM-1167
Dutch Treat		Epic 3269
East Coast Jazz #3		Bethlehem 1012
East Coast Jazz #8		Bethlehem 16
Les Elgart		Columbia 536
		594
		619
		684
		803
		875
		901
		979
		1108
Don Elliott	Mellophone	Bethlehem BCP-113
	Don Elliott Sings	Bethlehem BCP-15
	Title unknown	Bethlehem BCP-12
Ethel Ennis	Eyes for You	Victor LPM-2984
Gil Evans	The Gil Evans Orchestra	Verve V6-8838

The Tal Farlow Album
Maynard Ferguson
Stan Freeman
Barry Galbraith

Benny Goodman & Igor Stravinsky
Urbie Green

Johnny Guarnieri
Jimmy Hamilton and the New York Jazz Quintet
Coleman Hawkins

Reissued on CD

Reissued on CD

Neil Hefti

Billie Holiday

Lurlean Hunter

Jackie and Roy

Milt Jackson

Bobby Jaspar Quintet
Jazzband Having A Ball
Osie Johnson
Hank Jones
Thad Jones, Mel Lewis
Sheila Jordan
Morgana King

Pat Kirby
John LaPorta

Michael Legrand
John Lewis
Like Tweet
Joe Newman
The New Jazz Sound of Showboat
The Manhatten Jazz Septet
Marv Meridith
Jimmy McGriff

Into the Hot
The Individualism of Gil Evans

Screamin' Blues
The Music Man
Guitar and the Wind
Jazz Guitar Study Series
Guitar Improv
Guitar Comping
Play Along With Bach
Meeting at the Summit
Urbie Green Trombone & Rhythm 6-tet

The Coleman Hawkins Septet
The Hawk Flies High
Fantasy/Jazz Classics
Desafinado

Title unknown
Title unknown
Title unknown
Lil' Darlin
Title unknown
God Bless the Child
Reissued as CD
Lady in Satin
Reissued as CD B00004SGN5
Last Recording
Night Life
Lonesome Gal
Blue and Sentimental
Jackie and Roy
The Glory of Love
Ballads & Blues
Jazz n' Samba

A Bit of the Blues
The Talented Touch
Central Park North
Portrait of Sheila
Title unknown
Morgana King Sings the Blues
What is This Thing Called Love
3 Moods

Legrand Jazz
The John Lewis Piano

The Midgets

Strings (and all that) Jazz
The Big Band

Impulse A-9
Verve V-8555
Norgran MGN-19
Mainstream MRL-316
Columbia 1120
Decca DL-9200

Weybridge 0903
Weybridge 0902
Weybridge 0901
Columbia ML-6205
Victor LPM-1969
Command RS-857
Coral 57085

Urania 1204
Riverside 3049
Riverside ?
B000000Y1K
Impulse AS-28
UNI/ImpulseB000003N9W
Capital T-819
Victor 1287
Vik 1059
20th Century TFM 3139
Epic 3187
Columbia G-30782
K-Tel B000000RU9
CBS 450 883 2
Sony/Columbia

Verve 835-370-2
Vik LX-1061
Victor LPM-1151
Atlantic SD-1344
Storyville LP-322
ABC-Paramount 120
Atlantic 1242
Impulse AS-70
Columbia FPX –123
Dot DLP-9005
Victor LPM-1369
Capitol T-1044
Impulse A9
Blue Note BL-9002
EmArcy 36079
Mercury MG-20231
Decca DL-8428
Debut 122
EmArcy EXPR-1038
Columbia CL-1250
Atlantic 1272
Columbia CL-1618
Vik 1060
Columbia CS 8216
Coral CRL-57090
Strand SLS-1003
Solid State 18001

Artist	Title	Label
Hal McKusick	Jazz at the Academy	Coral 57116
	In A Twentieth Century Drawing Room	Victor LPM 1164
	Hal McKusick Quartet	Bethlehem BCP-16
	Hal McKusick Octet	Victor LPM 1164
	RCA Victor Jazz Workshop	Victor LPM 1366
Ted McNabb	Big Band Swing	Epic LN-366
Carmen McRae	Haven't We Met	Mainstream S-6044
	Second to None	Mainstream S- 6028
	Mad About the Man	Stanyan SR-10115
The Mello Sound		Decca DL 9208
Mellow Moods of Jazz		Victor LPM 1365
Helen Merrill	Dream Of You	Epic 36078
		Epic 36006
		Epic 36051
Debby Moore	My Kind of Blues	TopRank RM 310
Morgana King Sings the Blues		Mercury MG-20231
Sam Most Sextet	Doubles in Jazz	Jazztone J1256
	The Sam Most Sextette	Bethlehem BCP-18
Mark Murphy	Meet Mark Murphy	Decca DL-8390
	Rah	Riverside RLP-305
Music Minus One		MMO J4
Helen O'Connell	Green Eyes	VIK LX-1093
Chico O'Farrill	Nine Flags	Impulse A-9135
The Passion Guitars		Solid State 18007
Bucky Pizzarelli Guitar Quintet		Monmouth Evergreen
	MES-7066	
Tito Puente	Puente Goes Jazz	Victor 1312
Joe Puma		Bethlehem 1012
The Rhythm Section		Epic LN 3271
The Rhythm Section + One		Epic LN 3297
Willie Rodriguez	Flatjacks	Riverside RLP-469
George Russell	Jazz Workshop	Victor LPM-1312
	Reissued on CD	BMG KOC CD-7850
	New York, N.Y.	Decca DL-9216
	Jazz in the Space Age	Decca DL-9219
Aaron Sachs		Bethlehem 1008
Gunther Schuller, George Russell	Modern Jazz Concert	Columbia WL-127
Tommy Shepard		Coral 57110
Jimmy Smith	Bashin': The Unpredictable Jimmy Smith	Verve V6-8474
	Hoochie-Coochie Man	Verve V-8667
	Poinciana	Bethlehem BCP-22
Smith-Glamann Quintet	Swinging on a Harp	Mercury ??
		ABC 116
Special Delivery	Encores	Columbia CL 6164
Claude Thornhill	??	Kapp ??
	??	Kapp ??
	Snowfall	Monmouth-Evergreen
	MR6606	
	The Memorable Claude Thornhill	Columbia KG-32906
	Claude Thornhill and His Orchestra	Columbia 38224
		Trend TL 1002
		Insight IN 207
		Design DLP-106
Dinah Washington	For Those in Love	EmArcy MG-36011
	Reissued on CD	Polygram 314 514 073-2
	The Swingin' Miss D	EmArcy MG-36104
	Reissued on CD	Polygram 314 558 074-2
Margaret Whiting	Past Midnight	MGM E/SE-4006